Blossoms of Praise a 30 Day Journey

Written and Illustrated
Design Layout by Jan Asleson

ISBN 9780578639222

Library of Congress Control
   Number 2020901536

Printed in the United States of America by Ingram Spark/Lightning Source

Published by Spirit Wings Designs 2020
Independence KS
daslpacker55@yahoo.com

Visit at: www.spiritwingsdesigns.com

Blossoms of Praise

a 30 Day Journey

Created by

Jan Asleson

Blossom - the flower of a
seed plant, a stage of
development, to thrive,
to flourish

Praise - to worship, to express
admiration and thanks,
an expression of gratitude,
to honor, to confess

Dedication

Dedicated to Vaneetha
Rendall Risner

who

Dances
In The Rain

Acknowledgements

Thanks to Sheryl Runyon for
her wonderful editing skills and Praise
Testimony, also thanks to Hannah
Risner, Melanie Smith, Stacey
Risner and Jane Fisher Snyder
for your Praise Testimonies.
May our God richly reward you!

Forward

One day in May of last year, while perusing the internet looking for silk scarf design inspiration, I came across an art form I had never heard of - Eco Dyeing (also known as Botanical Printing). I had become skilled in the Serti technique of dyeing silk - incorporating my designs and artistic paintings onto silk using high quality dyes.

Eco Dying is something relatively new in the Textile Art world. It involves imprinting flowers, leaves, and other botanicals onto natural fibers, silk, wool, linen, hemp, cotton and bamboo. Not much has been written about the process of imprinting other than some general basics, you can take an online course or two but they can be expensive.

I was hooked! I looked forward to creating with this new process. I am blessed to live on property that is surrounded by 80 acres of woods which provides an endless supply of materials to experiment with. So, the next few months were spent gathering leaves, flowers, seeds, pods, berries and other plant materials.

As I began experimenting with silk and linen, rusted iron and vinegar, and natural dyes - Tannin, Osage Orange, Cutch, Indigo, Himalayan Rhubarb and Madder - creativity took over! Each individual creation was a treasure unfolding - its color and designs exclusive from each other.

I have always been drawn to God's Creative Diversity and Beauty, desiring to partake in and celebrate that part of His name. As I was reflecting on that, I heard the words "Blossoms of Praise" and imagined this book coming into existence. The art on the Praise pages are images that I imprinted on silk and linen using the new Eco Dye process.

As a natural seed is the beginning of a blossom, so praise to God is our spiritual seed sown to blossom as we savor the fruit of intimacy with Him, including love, joy, peace, patience, self-control, and all the attributes of who He is.

As you begin your journey each day, a praise verse will focus your heart and mind toward God. While you meditate on the daily verse, a Blossom of Praise of your own can be written in the space below the verse. Every 5th day, a Praise Testimony will encourage you to continue your journey.

My hope and prayer is that as you put your trust in God, He will bring to pass His will for your life and, as you proceed on this 30 - day Journey, that you will experience Him in new and deeper ways Blossoming into the Beautiful Creation that you are.

Jan Asleson

Abelia Mardi Gras

I will spend my life praising You, and singing high praises to You, my God, every day of my life !

Psalm 146:2 TPT

Today I praise God for ❧✻

Blackberry Leaves

I will proclaim the name of the Lord.
Oh praise the greatness of our God !

Deuteronomy 32:3   NIV

Today I praise God for 🌼

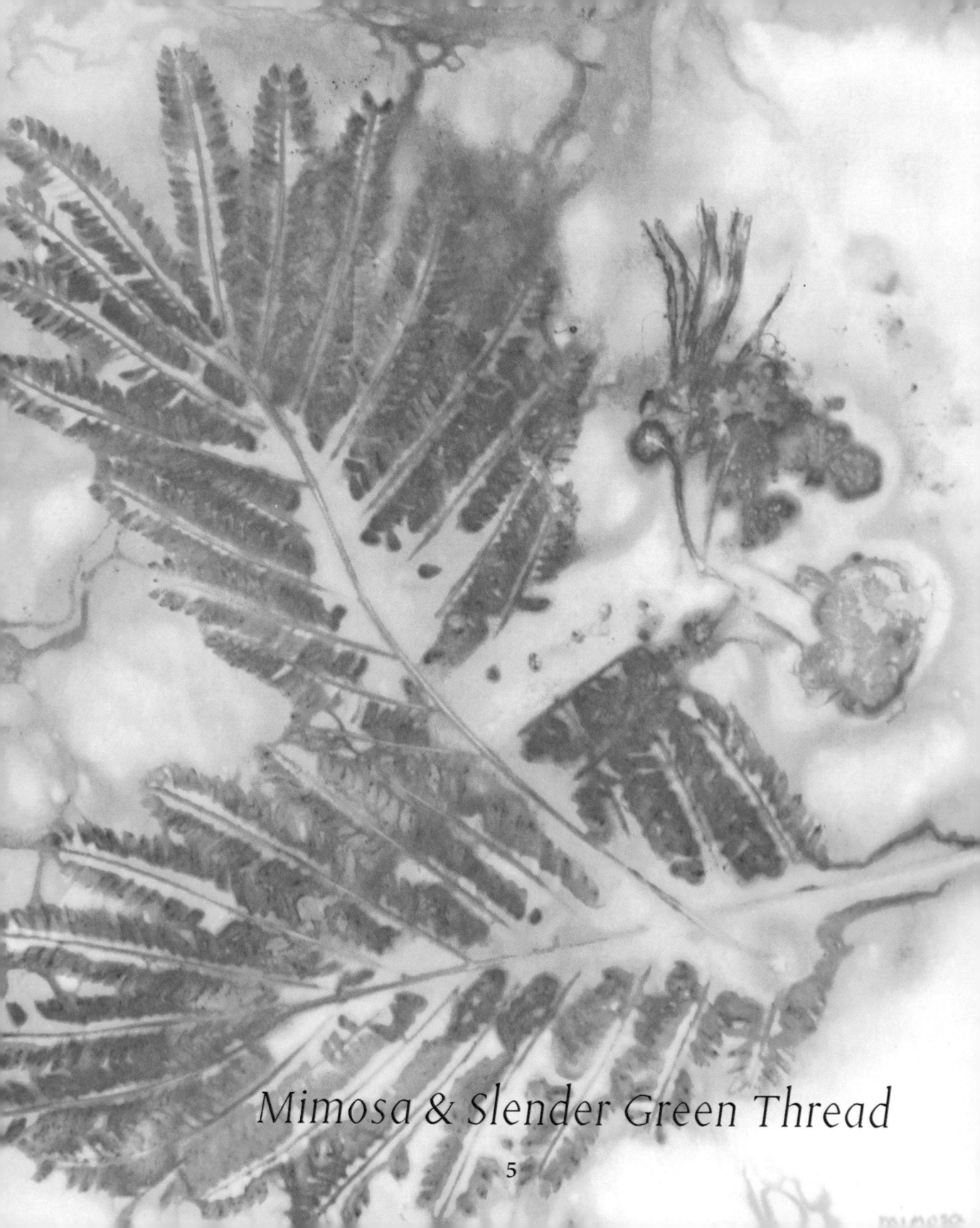

Mimosa & Slender Green Thread

I will bless and praise the Lord with my whole heart ! Let all His works throughout the earth, wherever His dominion stretches, let everything bless the Lord !

Psalm 103:22 TPT

Today I praise God for

Sunflower Leaves

7

So then, my soul, why would you be depressed?
Why would you sink into despair? Just keep
hoping and waiting on God, your Savior. For
no matter what, I will still sing with praise, for
living before His face is my saving grace!

Psalm 42:5   TPT

Today I praise God for ❧ ✼

Clematis

I will be fully satisfied as with the richest of foods; with singing lips my mouth will praise you. Psalm 63:5 NIV

Today I praise God for

We wanted a big family. While in our second year of marriage, we felt God impress on us six names. About a year and a half after our first child was born, we got pregnant again. We could not have been more excited and we prayed that our young daughter would somehow grasp that she was going to be a big sister. She showed very subtle signs that she was picking up on the upcoming change.

That's when it all went wrong. I began miscarrying while three hours away from home. I lay in the back of the van all the way home begging God to please spare us this loss. It was a blow to that sense of promise of having several children named by God but I was trying to be open to what He might be trying to whisper to me. As I tearily stared out at the sunny skies, a vivid picture of His hands holding that precious curly-haired life appeared in the clouds. I tried desperately to surrender to whatever His plan was but found myself just begging all the more.

The next morning my heavy-hearted husband and sweet young daughter went to church and left me home to rest. As I settled into a warm bath, I was startled by the start of contractions. No, this couldn't be! I think I was still solidly holding onto the promise, not the Promise-Giver. As each contraction washed over me, a wave of reality and softening surrender would sweep deeper into my clenched resolve that it would not end this way.

Upon delivering the amniotic sac intact, I held my baby and a unbidden song of praise welled up through my tear-choked voice. I found myself singing, "I love you, Lord, and I lift me voice, to worship You, O my soul, rejoice. Take joy my King, in what you hear, may it be a sweet, sweet sound in your ear." As I rocked that little life and sang to our Creator, a peace that passes all understanding came over me, a deep soothing flowing over and through my entire being and all felt as though it was as it should be.

I didn't ask God for anything further. My heart ached but He had so lovingly given me the physical, mental, and emotional stamina to make it through that event, allowing me to hold my baby and sing to Him. I was grateful and He had given me immense shalom peace.

That would have been enough but as I walked through the days of initial grief, He continued to shower His provision and reassurance over us. He prompted offers to bring us meals or to take our daughter so I could have space to process. He brought a sense of validity that this life did exist and had purpose by prompting us to name him and speaking confirmation through our closest friends. A friend painted a keepsake box for me to store his story, my thoughts, and letters to him over the coming years and it was covered in those fluffy clouds that had so spoken to me at the onset.

Later, while driving, spying my young daughter in the rearview mirror, I asked the Lord to help her understand that she wasn't going to have a baby brother after all. She peered out the window at the billowing clouds and broke into a grin and a little squeal while clapping her hands. She knew he was where he needed to be. And I knew. He had taken care of it all.

Stacey Risner

— · ❁ · —

Dogwood

I will forever praise this God who didn't close His heart when I prayed and never said no when I asked Him for help. He never once refused to show me His tender love.

Psalm 66:20 TPT

Today I praise God for

Roses with Leaves

15

Praise be to the Lord my Rock, who trains my hands for war, my fingers for battle.

Psalm 144:1 NIV

Today I praise God for

Woodland Fern

My mouth is filled with your praise, declaring your splendor all day long.

Psalm 71:8 NIV

Today I praise God for

Osage Orange

Lord, you are my God; I will exalt You and praise your name, for in perfect faithfulness You have done wonderful things, things planned long ago.   Isaiah 25:1 NIV

Today I praise God for ✄❀

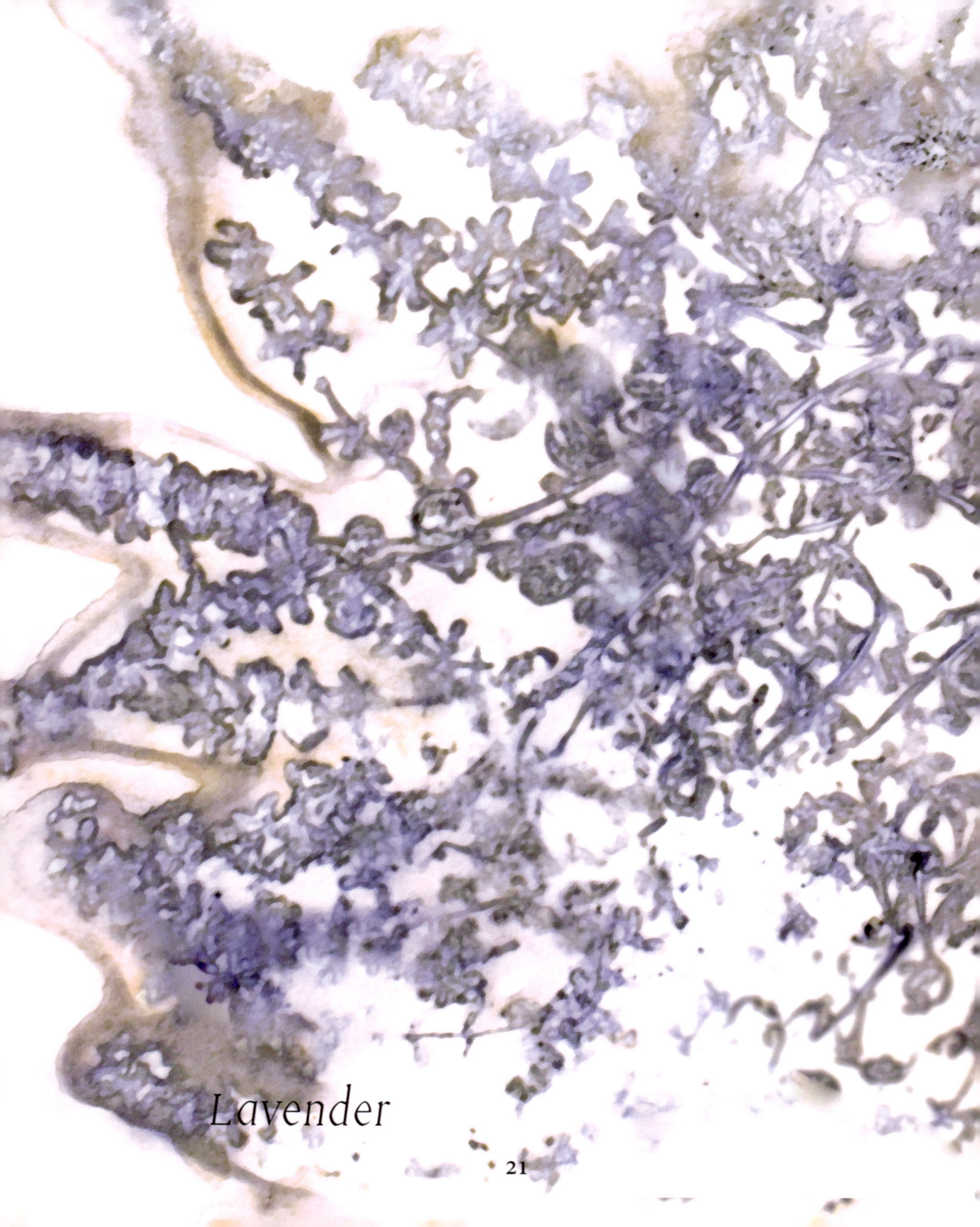

Lavender

Lord! I am bursting for joy over what you've done for me! My lips are full of perpetual praise.   .   Psalm 34:1 TPT

Today I praise God for ❧※

My dear and long- time Friend, Jan, asked me to write a "Blossoms of Praise" experience for her newest book by that title. I had a few ideas, but nothing gelled. I was going through a slump period of time - something strange and different to me - my strength had disappeared; sadness had taken hold during a significant life change, and my energy was exhausted. I struggled with it. I talked to God about it. I frustrated over it. I let Jan know that I wasn't sure that I was going to be able to fulfill her request. (However, the Lord knew the plan and the timing.)

I'd been asking: Lord, please, help me understand why I am feeling so low and depleted of energy, on top of the recent intensification of Fibro-myalgia and other physical health challenges I live with. I had been mulling this, contemplating this, having multiple conversations with Him about this. Even in the sacrifice of praise, joy seemed elusive. However, He doesn't always answer us right away.

Then, just about a week ago, one morning as I was struggling to even get out of bed and stand up - I began asking again for Grace and help. My strength, energy, and tenacity felt totally depleted. This word came to me very strongly and definitively: Transition.

Well, as a woman and a mother who had given birth to two sons, I immediately recalled how I felt during transition. That time was awful. That time was painful. That time was tearful. That time was emotional. That time felt like it would never end. I wanted it to hurry up and be over. It was exhausting!

Transition has been going on for several months and includes moving from a 3-bedroom house to fulltime living in a 42' RV which provides numerous physical challenges for me. However, this Transition, I believe, is related to the plan and purpose that God has for my husband and I.

This morning, January 3, 2020, as I awoke from the first decent night's sleep in many days, I realized I felt better. A bit chipper even! The Holy Spirit reminded me of the compositions He led me to create when Fibro-myalgia, chronic fatigue, and carpal tunnel syndrome became fullblown and debilitating in 2010. I shall get that notebook out again and read through the things the Holy Spirit spoke to me to write and remind myself of The Refreshing that comes through our Relationship with Jesus. He is the Living Water.

Saturday, January 11, 2020: The Holy Spirit has been speaking to me, reminding me, and I've written some new things since I submitted the first writing of this. Isn't that just like God. Our story is never finished until He calls us home. Times and seasons continue. Many times, though, trouble, difficulty, and pain can seem to dominate. These words were spoken to my heart this morning:

"When Troubles Assail
　Let Praise Avail:"

I knew this, but it took on a much more powerful meaning this morning. I meditated on those words. I sensed a connection to a song. I Googled the words. "Standing on the Promises of God" came up on the website hymnal.net, under the 'Classic' tab - one of my favorite songs we sang in the church I attended while growing up.
The second verse:

"Standing on the promises that cannot fail,
　When the howling storms of doubt and fear assail,
　By the living Word of God I shall prevail,
　Standing on the promises of God."

What a beautiful reminder and confirmation!

Sheryl Runyon

Pansy Redbud & Pods

*Praise be to the name of God for ever
and ever; wisdom and power are His.*

Daniel 2:20 NIV

Today I praise God for ❧✺

Maple & Rose

I will praise You because I am fearfully and wonderfully made; Your works are wonderful, I know that full well.

Psalm 139:14 NIV

Today I praise God for

Walnut Leaves

29

The Lord is my strength and my shield; my heart trusts in Him, and He helps me. My heart leaps for joy, and with my song I praise Him.   *Psalm 28:7 NIV*

Today I praise God for

Sumac, Oak & Persimmon

31

Praise be to the Lord, to God our Savior,
who daily bears our burdens.

Psalm 68:19 NIV

Today I praise God for

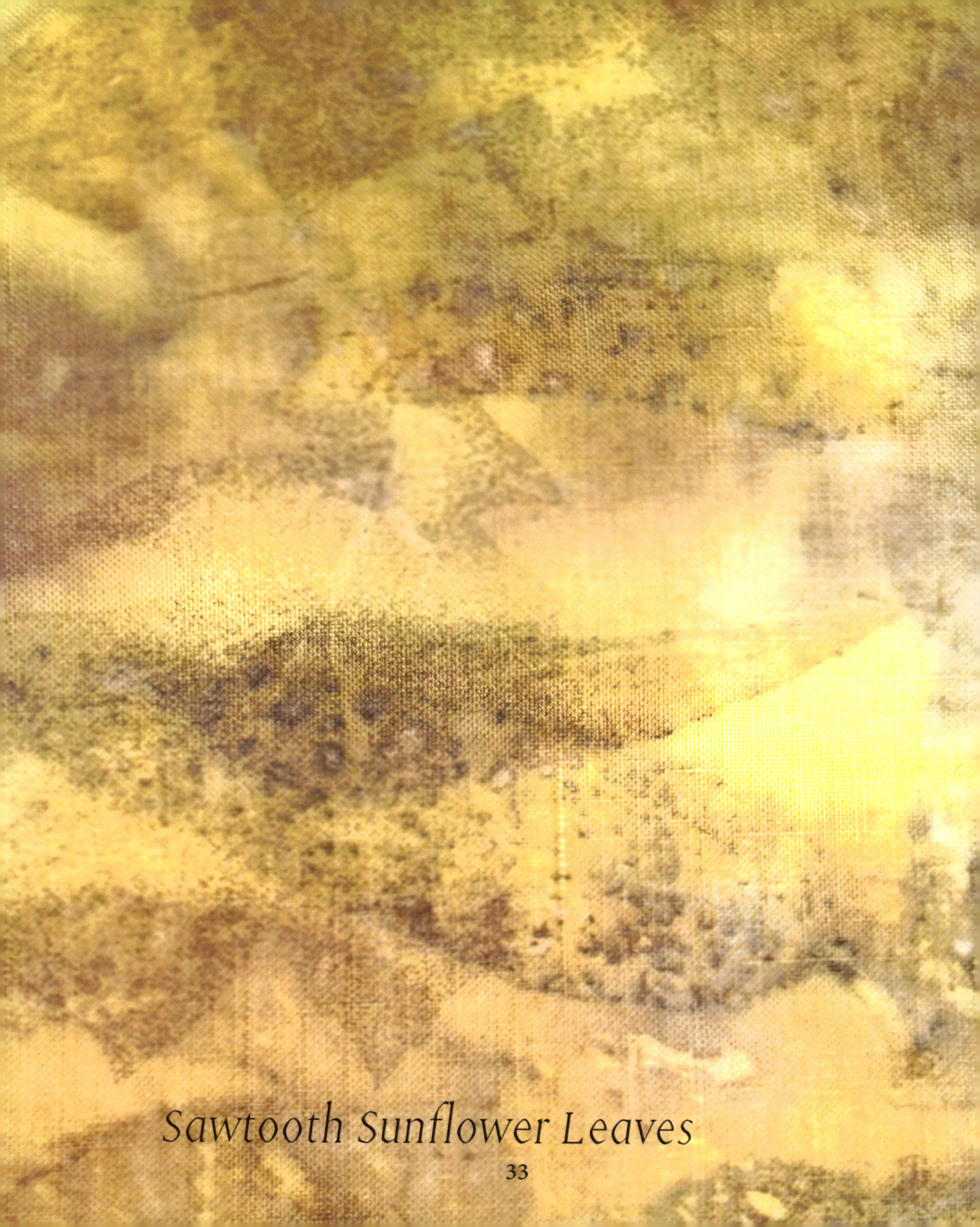

Sawtooth Sunflower Leaves

Heal me, Lord, and I will be healed; save me and I will be saved, for you are the one I praise. Jeremiah 17:14 NIV

Today I praise God for ❧✺

The rental house was being sold. I gave God an earful while sitting on the porch. Tears streamed down my face. Fervently, I pleaded: "Please don't make us move. We've moved so many times. My kids need stability." God heard, but we still had to move.

I was so tired of renting and moving. A friend suggested I consider purchasing a home. As a single Mom with four children, it didn't seem like a possibility. The search began for a new place to live. A friend showed me a two bedroom house that was going to be auctioned on Saturday. It was half the size of the one we currently lived in.

"Really God! This can't be where you want us to live! It's small. It's only two bedrooms! Where am I going to sleep?" "Trust Me." God said. I chose to trust Him. Through the favor of a friend, I was approved for a set dollar amount for the house. I prayed. I asked God to make it very clear to me as to whether or not this was to be our new home and to shut the door if not.

On Saturday, I went to the auction, got my number, and patiently waited as the contents of the house were auctioned off. I kept eyeing the people going in and out, wondering how many had more money than I. My budget wasn't much, but it was what I could afford.

Finally, it was time to sell the house. My nerves were getting the best of me. I'd never tried to purchase anything at an auction, let alone, a house! The realtor asked everyone who was interested in the house to come over. I looked around, sizing everyone up, noticing that I was the only one with a number. "Could it possibly be?" "Was I really the only person who was interested in bidding on this house?"

The bid opened. I raised my number. He upped the bid and looked around. Nobody! Not one other person responded. I was the only one who had bid on the house! And, I had just purchased it way under budget.

I was in Awe. God heard and answered my prayers. He knew, much more than I, what we needed. That day was a "Yes." Often we think of unanswered prayers as a "No." However, that's not always the case. Sometimes, it's because He has something much better for us.

There was no question in my mind after that. He had made it very clear to me that the house was for me and that I serve a Loving Father who takes care of His children. "Thank you, Lord, for taking such good care of me even when it seems like you are not."

It was tough for awhile, sleeping on the bottom of a bunk bed in a room with my two girls. I praised God though. I knew I was right where I needed to be, I was thankful.

A year later, a gentleman from our church asked me if I had an attic. I said "Yes, I do." He said "Well, the Lord is telling me to build you a bedroom. Do you need a bedroom?" I was speechless! He built a bedroom at no charge except for materials.

I didn't have money for materials. But, again, God provided every single penny that was needed. I didn't have to borrow the money or put it on a credit card.

Philippians 4:19 says: "And my God will meet all your needs according to the riches of His Glory in Christ Jesus."

Hannah Risner

Zinnia

Sing to God, sing in praise of His name,
extol Him who rides on the clouds; rejoice
before Him - His name is the Lord.

Psalm 68:4 NIV

Today I praise God for

Trumpet Vine & Blackberry

Enter His gates with thanksgiving and His courts with praise; give thanks to Him and praise His name.   Psalm 100:4 NIV

Today I praise God for ✦❋

Persimmon & Coleus

But I, with shouts of grateful praise, will sacrifice to you. What I have vowed I will make good. I will say, "Salvation comes from the Lord."　　　　　　Jonah 2:9 NIV

Today I praise God for ❧✿

Redbud & Eucalyptus

43

The Lord lives! Praise be to my Rock!
Exalted be my God, the Rock, my
Savior! 11 Samuel 22:47 *NIV*

Today I praise God for

Oak

I will be glad and rejoice in You; I will sing the praises of Your name, Oh Most High.   Psalm 9:2 NIV

Today I praise God for ❧✽

In the past few years the Lord has led me on a journey about praise and the powerful tool it is for our lives. I want to share a part of that journey where He has led me concerning praise and barrenness. This has been a process and I have in no terms "arrived." I am continuing to learn and grow day by day in its application.

Isaiah 54 is my personal "life" scripture. I have clung to this chapter, especially Isaiah 54:1, because I was unable to have children. Thankfully, I saw this promise fulfilled. The Lord brought me a husband with children.

More recently, the Lord brought a deeper application for these scriptures. I realized barrenness is not only being childless, but there is spiritual barrenness a person can experience too. I identify spiritual barrenness as seasons when you don't have a harvest where you have spiritually sowed, or any place you do not see spiritual fruit or life.

My husband and I were walking through a dormant and unfruitful season with our church. It had decreased in numbers. There had been a pruning and now we were in a season where we seemingly saw no growth. We knew there was more for us, but the way was unclear on how to get there.

During this challenging time, I attended a conference. A woman shared from Isaiah 54:1-3. The Lord directed her to this scripture after struggling for months with insomnia. The Lord spoke to her that praise was significant to this battle. He showed her that praise would bring her into His presence where He could strengthen her faith. Additionally, her praise would allow Him to work supernaturally - just as it did for the barren woman in Isaiah 54. As she began to praise God in this battle, she was healed from insomnia.

I realized this was what I needed to do. I knew this situation needed to be in God's hands for Him to work. Praising was my way to give it to Him and open the door for His changes. I was grateful for this direction and to learn how to live this truth in my life. God was wanting to teach me Habakkuk 3:17-18.

Almost two years after I attended the conference, at the beginning of 2019, my husband said the Lord told him this was "the year of breakthrough" for the church. I was not expecting anything to change overnight.

To my surprise, in January, we began to have new people at our church. The church atmosphere changed and the Lord's presence began manifesting in new and special ways in both our Sunday and Wednesday services. We were amazed. My husband and I would say after a service that it was so awesome we didn't want it to end. We couldn't wait till the next service.

God was faithful. 2019 ended with significant changes for our church. The Lord showed us how to sow praise into barrenness and spiritually allow God to work His changes. We believe we have not seen the full harvest of our praise. We know we are in a new season and we are expectant of greater things to come.

Praise will allow Him to move in your barrenness.

Melanie Smith

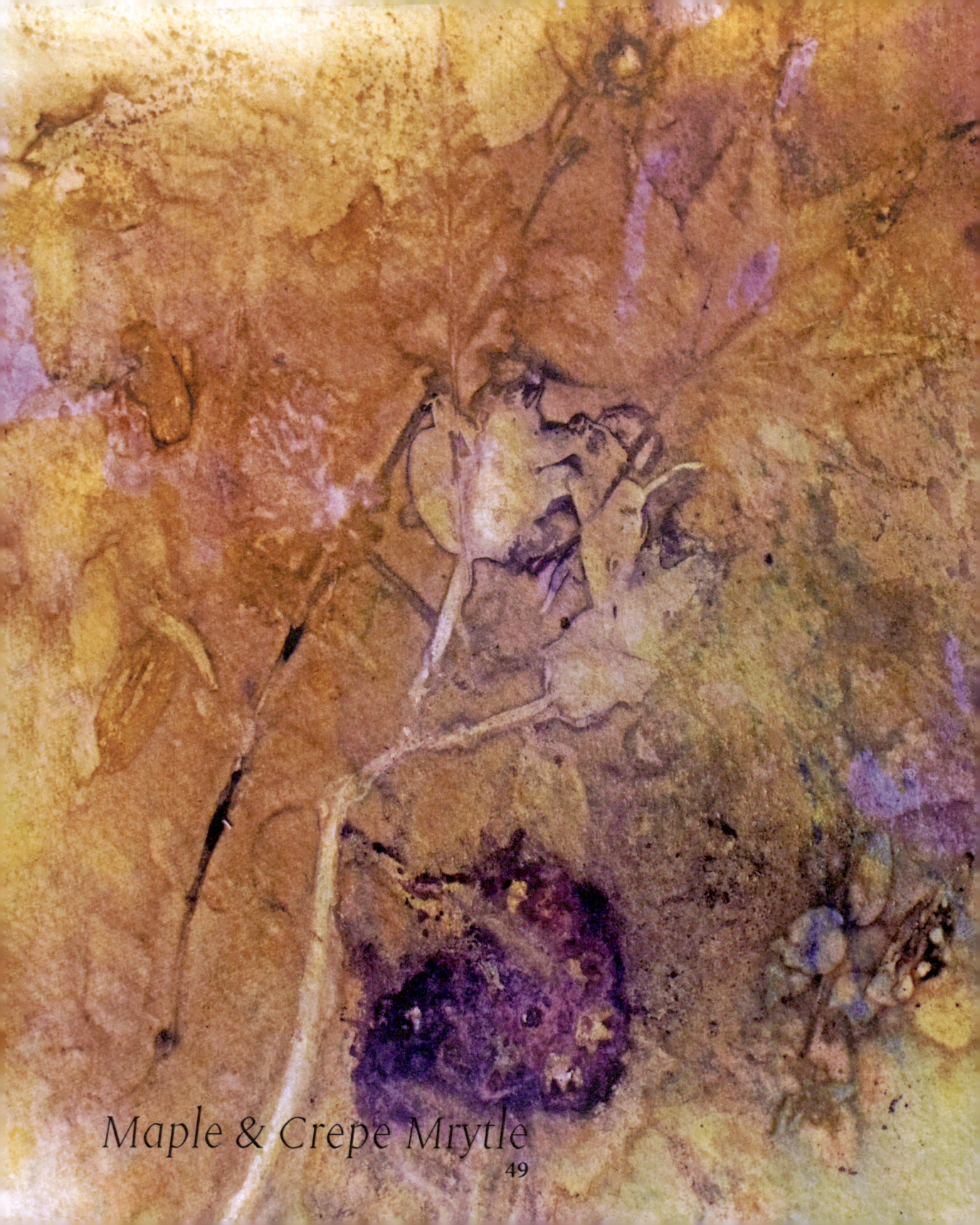

Maple & Crepe Mrytle

Praise be to the God and Father of our Lord Jesus Christ, the Father of compassion and the God of all comfort.

11 Corinthians 1:3 NIV

Today I praise God for

Hydrangea

The Lord is my strength and my shield; my heart trusts in Him, and He helps me. My heart leaps for joy, and with my song I praise Him.   *Psalm 28:7* NIV

Today I praise God for

Japanese Maple

Because your love is better than life, my lips will glorify you. I will praise You as long as I live, and in Your name I will lift up my hands.   Psalm 63:3-4 NIV

Today I praise God for

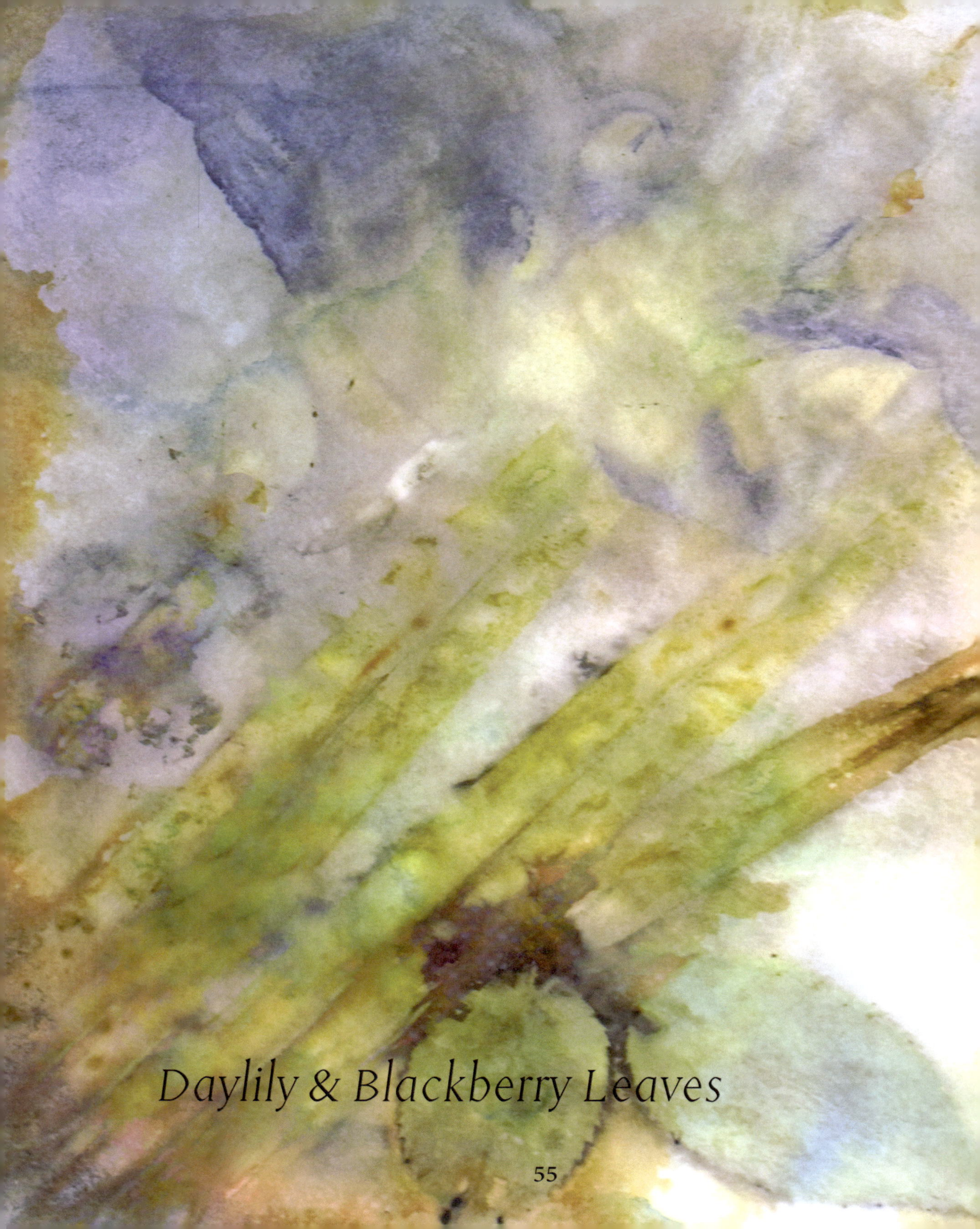

Daylily & Blackberry Leaves

*Praise be to the Lord, for He has heard my
cry for mercy.*   Psalm 28:6 NIV

Today I praise God for ❧❋

Coral Bells

Praise Him for His miracles of might! Praise Him for His magnificent greatness!

Psalm 150:2 TPT

Today I praise God for ❧❈

Unfortunately, it was a day similar to what many parents have experienced: our sixteen year old daughter announced that she was moving out. She decided that she no longer wanted to live by our rules. She was moving in with a friend and her family. I was stunned! I watched as she drove away. I felt helpless. I felt hopeless. I knew this was the path the enemy wanted her to take - a path of destruction and death.

As a desperate mother, who had a personal relationship with Jesus and who read my Bible, I had often quoted scripture without really believing for change. I set my face like a flint, determined to pursue that relationship in greater measure. He had the power to save and turn lives around! Now, as I read God's Word, I asked Him to show me verses that would change this situation (and me).

Every night, I met with Jesus to read the Bible, listen for the Holy Spirit's leading, and write down scriptures. I would say them out loud. I memorized them. The first scripture was Romans 4: 19-21. Abraham had received what seemed like an impossible promise, but He trusted and did not waiver. He was convinced God would do what He said. Ezekiel did not waiver. He followed God's instructions and spoke and prophesied life into dry bones {dry situations}. Reading God's Word with Expectation for myself and my family became Exciting!

Human reasoning and eyes on the circumstances can be debilitating. It can bring fear and doubt. I was so tempted to keep looking at the situations in others' lives that did not turn out well. Fear would try to set in when the phone calls came: she was in jail; she was having uncontrollable thoughts of suicide. God told me to stop looking at those things. He told me to put "blinders" on - to keep my eyes on His Word, His Truth, and to take captive the thoughts that caused me to doubt rather than trust and believe.

It seemed the more I learned the more things came my way that required me to put what I had learned into action. It was necessary to recognize that these things were sent as an attempt to destroy my daughter. Then, I thanked God for all the times (listing them out loud) that He led me in victory over my enemies. After that, I eagerly sought the answer in God's Word. The Holy

Spirit always brought verses alive and they filled me with hope. Finally, against all reasoning, I would start thanking and praising God!

Fifteen years later, I was a changed person. God provided everything He had promised me. Through all the drug addiction, arrests, suicide prevention, and all that goes with those things, God did miraculous things for me, my daughter and my family. He never let me down. He is truly a Rewarder of those who seek Him.

1 John 5:14-15 became one of my favorite scripture passages: (14) "This is the confidence we have in approaching God: that if we ask anything according to His will, He hears us. (15) And if we know that He hears us - whatever we ask - we know that we have what we asked of Him."

When you seek Him, expect Him to do the impossible if needed, and wait...you will not be disappointed. Never give up and don't let circumstances determine your truth. Expect that God has the power to do what He has promised and then just praise and wait!!!

Jane Fisher Snyder

✻✽✻✽

Crepe Mrytle

61

I will sing the Lord's praise, for He has
been good to me. Psalm 13:6 *NIV*

Today I praise God for ❧✺

Red Crepe Mrytle

The way you counsel and correct me makes me praise You more, for Your whispers in the night give me wisdom showing me what to do next. Psalm 16:7 TPT

Today I praise God for

Celosia

For Your tender mercies mean more to me than life itself. How I love and praise You, God!   Psalm 63:3 TPT

Today I praise God for ❧✻

Black Eyed Susan
Wild Rose Leaves

He put a new song in my mouth, a hymn of praise to our God. Many will see and fear the Lord and put their trust in Him.

Psalm 40:3 TPT

Today I praise God for ❧❀

Begonia

Praise the Lord. Blessed are those who fear the Lord, who find great delight in His commands.

Psalm 112:1 NIV

Today I praise God for ❧❀

In 1985, when I was 28, my husband David and I were the Park Managers of a 2000-acre private Christian community in the mountains in Colorado. Shortly after moving there, I had a series of dreams and visions concerning a property with a few cabins hidden in the woods. In the dreams/visions, I saw God's light radiating there. Hurt and wounded people came. They were set free. They were being transformed to be and do all that God had created them for. As I saw these things, I heard the spiritual name of the place: "Shiloh"- the interpretation being "a place of God's rest."

The revelation took place over a week of time. I was so excited by this God encounter! I shared what I had seen and heard with a seasoned Christian woman who had written books about her journeys with God. Her response to me was: "Are you willing to wait for God's timing on bringing these things to pass, even if it is five, ten, twenty, or even thirty years from now?" I was indignant at her response! I was sure it was going to happen very soon!

We left Colorado after a year, moved to Wisconsin for a time, then traveled on the road with David's job. Every new place we traveled through found me looking for the land I had seen back in 1985.

Four years later, my Grandma Shryock passed away. She left me her one-carat diamond engagement ring. I had just lost my engagement ring, flushed down a drain. As it disappeared, I heard God say to me,"Praise me. Thank me." I had no idea that God had a replacement for me that superseded the ring I had. As I put Grandma's ring on, the Holy Spirit revealed to me that, in the same way He had given me the ring, He would give me the land He had shown me in 1985.

As years went by, I experienced many losses: my Mom died in a car accident, we lost our household possessions in a flood, we gave up our property and the home we were building to move in with and help my aging Dad, my husband took a lesser job to be available to help with Dad, and I walked through ovarian cancer.

In all of this, I always heard God say, "Trust me. Thank me. Praise me." Occasionally, during those years, I would think of the promise: the Shiloh vision and dream. I had let it go many times. Yet, it remained in my heart like a tiny spark. Shiloh had to do with legacy, family, destiny, and generational dreams.

My Grandma Shryock had worked at Keswick in New Jersey many summers as the camp registrar. Keswick was a place for missionaries to go and get refreshed, to connect and be spiritually encouraged. My parents had purchased eighty acres of woods in 1983 - my Mom had a dream of cabins on the property where weary souls could come to rest and to be refreshed.

January 1, 2015: As I sought God for my word for the year, I heard "Believe." "Believe what God?" I asked. "Do you believe I can give you the land?" "It's been 30 years," I replied. "I don't know if I can believe or not." He asked me again…."Yes Lord, I will commit to believe." I answered, with doubt in my heart. Months flew by as I thanked God and believed, though seeing nothing materialize.

Then, in October, through a series of events, the land we were living on while taking care of Dad - the eighty acres of woods that my Mom saw cabins on - was willed to us! This land superseded the land we had given up in 2006 to take care of Dad.

Fast forward to 2020 - I am still praising God and thanking Him for His plan and timing. During the last thirty-five years, I have learned to trust God's Goodness, His Timing, and to wait on Him in confident expectation of His Faithfulness. I am still learning. And, as I raise my voice to glorify Him, my very being is transformed into who He created me to be. In His season, He will orchestrate the cabins. He will send the people that need to experience transformation. He will continue to glorify His name in and through David and me as we give Him Praise!

"Stop imitating the ideals and opinions of the culture around you, but be inwardly transformed by the Holy Spirit through a total reformation of how you think. This will empower you to discern God's will as you live a beautiful life, satisfying and perfect in His eyes."   Romans 12:2 TPT

Jan Asleson

The Lord Almighty
Is His name.
And His power
is still the same.
He still does work
In a miraculous way,
Sometimes in
A single day.

Not by might
Or power, we know,
But by His Spirit
He does show
His sovereignty
In loving ways,
As we trust Him
with our days.

Great, awesome wonders
We do see
And our spirits
are set free.
So, Lord, we come
And worship Thee
With upraised hands
And bended knee.

Rusty Risner 1993

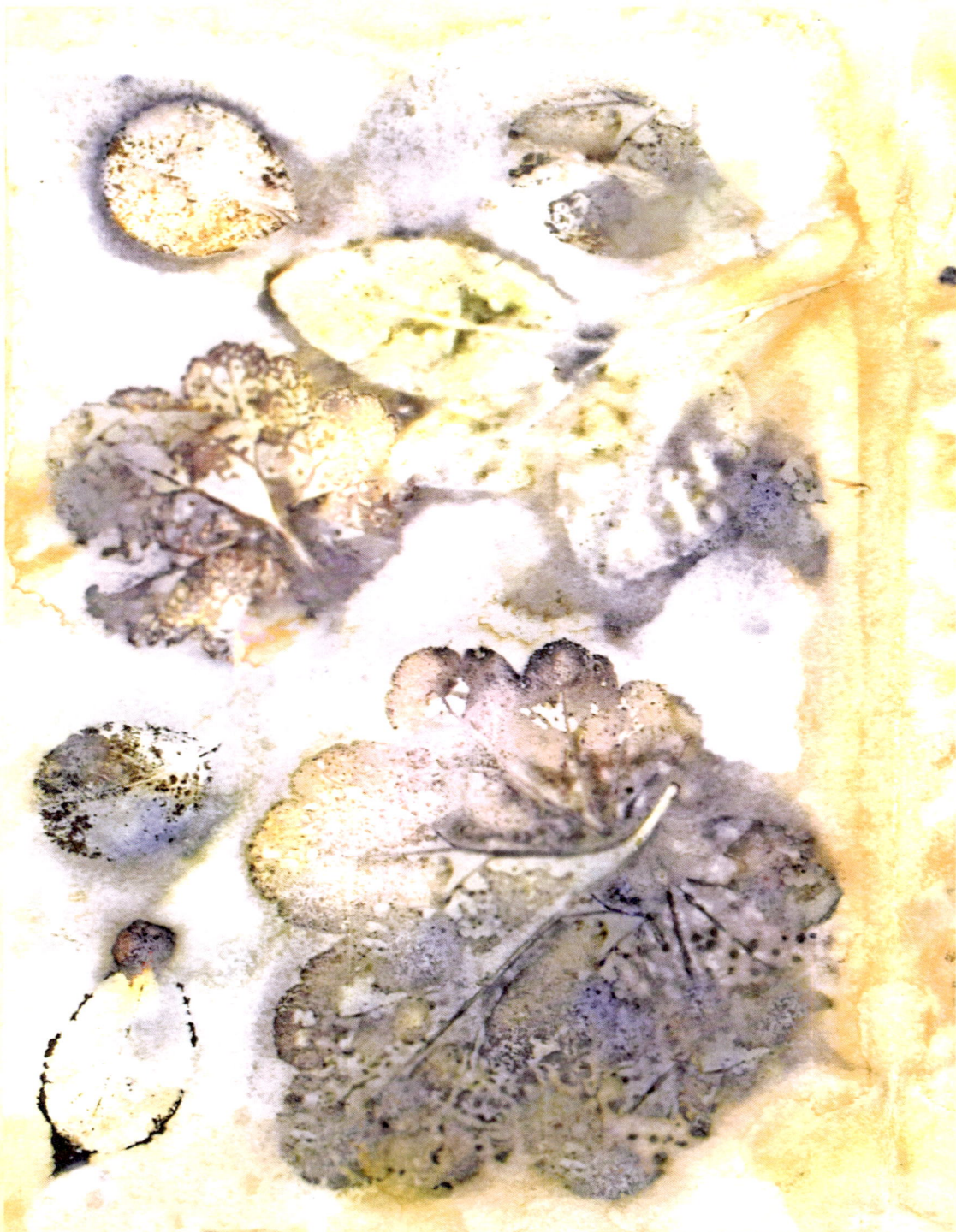

My Praise Testimonies

Jan Asleson - Author/Illustrator

My designs are inspired by a desire to share with others the beauty of God's Creation that I see around me. My passion is to encourage others through my artistic mediums to not give up on their dreams, to recognize the Blessings all around them and to know that there is always hope.

I find my creativity in many mediums including watercolor, oils, pastels, acrylics, jewelry design, metal work, book illustration work, silk art, textiles, and portraiture.

I live in South-East Kansas with my husband David, two Native American Indian dogs, a Mustang and Arabian horse.

You can find me at www.spiritwingsdesigns.com

www.ingramcontent.com/pod-product-compliance
Lightning Source LLC
Chambersburg PA
CBRC101141030426
42334CB00010B/123

* 9 7 8 0 5 7 8 6 3 9 2 2 2 *